WHISPERS
OF
VALIANCE

ABHISHEK SAMANTRAY

SIDDHARTH JEET

Woven Words Publishers OPC Pvt. Ltd.

Registered Office: Vill: Raipur, P.O: Raipur Paschimbar, Dist: Purba
Midnapore, Pin: 721401, West Bengal, India.
Branch Office(Operations): Hyderabad

www.wovenwordspublishers.com
Email: publish@wovenwordspublishers.com
First published by Woven Words Publishers OPC Pvt. Ltd., 2019

Copyright© Abhishek Samantray & Siddharth Jeet, 2019

POETRY

IMPRINT: WOVEN WORDS FIRE

ISBN 13: 978-93-88762-00-7
ISBN 10: 93-88762-00-2

Price: $ 6/ 200 INR

Printed and bound in India by Woven Words Publishers.

PREFACE

Poetry is by far the most underrated art form, because too many people think that poems are boring. They hear corny children's books, and assume that all poetry is that way. But music is poetry. RAP is poetry. Every song you've ever heard and love. It is hoped that the title-page of this work will sufficiently indicate it a general character, and render a lengthened preface unnecessary.

The poets trusts that while it may be found specially adapted for schools as a reading book in english poetry for the more advanced pupils, it may also be a welcome guest in the family and social circle; and thus be alike useful as a school-book or a pocket companion;-that it may in some degree deepen the love for country & its martyr, favor the love of national freedom, and the growth of true patriotism.

ACKNOWLEDGEMENTS

"Thanks to deceased martyrs of our country who encouraged us to write this poetry book.

Thanks to our English teacher Mr. Dilip Kumar Kezhakkeveetil who sparked the interest for English literature inside us.

Thanks to our parents & friends who left no stone unturned in assisting us while writing the poetries"

LIST OF POETRIES

AGES PAST: - "STRUGGLE"

Prologue – Tributary piece of poetry towards forefathers, who have struggled out for freedom

Ages past were built those monarchial battle of archery blocks.

Those that were proves of how our forefathers fought.

Those that they resembled our earlier bravery hearts.

Freedom that wasn't borrowed or bought instead was owned.

The country saw blood shredded crown.

The great White Mountains that were all dressed with blood sheet gown.

This hardship of freedom struggle wasn't at all easy indeed.

For whom to take care of either of the family or of the motherland first.

Being in such a worrifying moment they rather choose to serve the country's priority the most.

So, rose the brave warrior's heart for the enemies to get them the worst.

Bravely fought against the ravens & scavengers to teach them bitter lesson.

Those are the real men armed warriors of the nation.

MY SHARES OF EARTH

*Prologue – This piece of poetry is tribute to
Captain Vikram Batra, PVC was an officer of the
Indian Army, posthumously awarded with the
Param Vir Chakra, India's highest and most
prestigious award for valor, for his actions
during the 1999 Kargil War in Kashmir between
India and Pakistan. The poem reflects how he
fought even after being shot thus showing
ultimacy of courage.*

He received two shots of iron bullets in his chest.

That got his arteries pressed,

which eventually chocked off his breath.

Left bloodied all over his vest.

Pierced his brain for having a forever rest.

Severe pain that got his all veins being pricked.

Suddenly paleness & peculiar silence went on
everywhere.

That quietly led his legs shattered & dragged him to fall.

But again he gathered his breath & woke up with an instant call.

A call that was made by his own motherland.

Nevertheless, took on his gun.

Killed tens of demons until they were dead.

Thus proving himself the real army men.

The time has come now to wish you good bye.

May you be happy forever & ever.

Thus then reciting :-

"Oh , my motherland please fetch me my shares of earth".

Then felt the son all after losing his mournful breath.

Motherland responded raising her hand in all directions wide just to grab up her son in her lap.

Kudos 'ABHINANDAN'

Prologue - Abhinandan Varthaman is a wing-commander in the Indian Air Force. In the 2019 India-Pakistan standoff, he was held under captivity for 60 hours in Pakistan after his aircraft was shot down in an aerial dogfight. This poetry reflects about him.

Riding away the MIG- bison you flew through the terror's mansion.

Without hesitating for any bit of the present situation you better choose to concentrate on yours permitted mission.

F-16 that you targeted & just got it smashed with a missile's explosion.

High up in the air all the ways away from home, bravely punished the terrorists with bomb.

On safely getting own self ejected.

You laid down mistakenly in foreigner's den

& destroyed all documents of own self of not letting them in foreigner's hand.

Thus that was perfect decision by your keen brain.

You easily did the perfect locomotion.

You gave them a better tuition.

You taught them a better lesson.

A lesson that wouldn't ever can the civilians forget.

So, for generations yours bravery talks would bumble in every ears forever long.

The act you performed would pass from generation to generation & by on.

" O ABHINANDAN " .

Brave lion since the day that you were born.

Proud should be the motherland that's India where you belong.

This song is dedicated to you as a flaming song.

SOLDIERS ON MISSION

Prologue - Para (Special Forces), commonly known as Para SF, is the special operations unit of the Indian Army. They have executed various dangerous operation throughout the country when motherland gave them a call. This short poem is a tribute to their service.

They trekked through the mountains & denser den.

Knowing very well that death can arrive at any time, without asking anyone's name.

Getting amidst the harsh weather ever, for which not much air planes could easily fly.

From dusk to the dawn you walk kilometers no bar.

May be whatsoever the situations be

You always stood ready for any sorts of war.

Fear is just a pity thing for which you kept your heart in a hidden jar.

Your achievements count on your shoulders owing the stars.

You are not just our soldiers instead are the

great heroes of the soil those who have fought
many wars so far.

Your happier moments happens in the tests of
today's mission.

"CALL" TO SON

Prolouge - Second Lieutenant Arun Khetarpal, PVC (14 October 1950 – 16 December 1971) born in Pune, Maharashtra, was an officer of the Indian Army and a posthumous recipient of the Param Vir Chakra, India's highest military decoration for valour in face of the enemy. He was killed in action in the Battle of Basantar in the Battlefield of Shakargarh during the Indo-Pakistan War of 1971 where his actions earned him his honor. The poetry is a fictional event relating Arun Sir having a conversation with his mother.

Cring! Cring! The phone louds to get a swing.

Hello! Utters the son -

"Son, when are you being back to home?"
Interrogates mom.

Mom again:-

Proclaims yours beloved part & often weeps
hiding herself in the roomy timid.

With a letter pressed under her pillow over bed.

Faded are now the charming rooms light.

Even seems fainted day's twilight.

Hoping for your home coming i just wait by side
our gate peeping at the endless road fleet.

Just wandering round the house Myra often asks
about you.

Little Myra wishes that her Dad to be present on
her coming birthday's night.

With whom to share, with whom to discuss my
pain vanishes in all agony's flight.

"Son"

(Utters in a soary voice)

Mom I am fine -

It's not I don't just wanted to come

Instead it's actually the political loam

That compels us to withstand the bullets on our
chest's made foam.

Tell my part if I don't come it's only 'cuz I couldn't make it through.

Tell Myra unlike her father she just has to be

brave enough to bloom.

Mom make my little darling, princessly gowned on her date of bridal look.

Mom am there to take care of thousands son.

But, I promise to return home soon.

Either I would come with my nation's flag or be else wrapped in nation's flag as boon.

MOTHERLAND'S CALL

Prologue – This is a tributary poem to Mangal Pandey, India's official 1st freedom fighter who ignited the spark of 1857 freedom revolt in India. In this poetic context Mangal Pandey ji is addressing the young mass of Barackpore & tells them to contribute themselves towards patriotic movement.

Why does you sit idle in such blindfolded stone caged hut?

Letting yourself being addressed as blind.

Come out & taste the sunrise light.

When shall you wake up from your sleepy daylight's height?

Cries the country's soil, weeps the skies.

Can't you feel her pain, can't your ear hear those teary voice of her.

Indeed just for the sake of freeing up your country

The "war of freedom" even that was fought by

22

Laborers & farmers as well.

Tear & blood shades of fear sprinkled everywhere.

How many of such have been imprisoned have you
ever kept a record of them?

Calls for your wake up thine motherland to the
battle ground.

MOURNFUL WEEP

Prologue - A tributary song to soldiers who are martyred in Pulwama attack. Everyone weeps out, pays them tribute later take oath that all countrymen would stand as one against their common enemies.

Weeps tricolored flag on losing her own brave
soldier sons.

Cries even every civilian alike boats as if sailing in
the bloodied ocean.

Country's army men sacrificed their life on the
edges of foes knife.

Leaving all their belongings in an endless grief.

Mom's lappet got soaked up in heartfelt tears.

Even sleeplessness has laid its presence in
Daddy's eyes.

He urged to be back soon last time when came.

Alas! He won't ever return again 'cuz he boarded
to an aimless train.

Dear wife has lost herself in a mournful weep.

Little son cries for his Dad.

Even weeps our country land.

Such worrying gestures of astonishment could also
be depicted within trees of the mainland.

Blessed soldier son you are of the motherland.

Who, thus bravely have sacrificed their lives

for the sake of homeland.

Hail India, Hail India! Soars our tricolored flag.

Waving flag sings the song of victorious shag.

Dear lightening souls of the nation

Make up your mind, body, heart & soul all as one.

Come let's take oath against all our foes of forth.

We shouldn't give them any way thus get cleaned
up our rifle's nose.

LATENT SOLDIERS

Prologue – This piece of poetry is tribute towards brave espionage agency men of this country, who without bothering about their lives, work for the country as a latent soldier throughout their life.

Wars are won not only because of those that are physically fought.

Instead are won for someone who have allowed it all to be mindfully brought.

Wars are carried out not only because of those that are planned of.

Instead wars are carried for someone who really pledged to take care of.

Care of all about soil, take care of all about civilians.

They are the brave soldiers of the nation.

Who if found guilty always keeps numb, neither utters a penny against the nation; nor even losses any such information.

Always ready to be sacrificed of for any manifestation

But won't ever allow any such obstruct causing to disturb an operation.

Such misery is that even out of having his beautiful name.

He is always referred sometimes as spy or at times as an agent.

His life almost swirls amongst within hide & seek policy.

Being least bothered about these stupid things.

He better focuses on leading life in utmost free.

Sometimes here in nation, sometimes there in far destination.

This is what is he's daily's investigation.

Self- prepared never off duty hence always

in seek of new information's for the sake of profiting the nation.

Yes, he is the hidden soldier of the nation.

Migrating, immigrating whirling all around whose
life is often led in dangerous whirlpool
configuration.

All my countrymen's let's hail at least for these
who are part of segregation.

WE ARE THE DEAD

Prologue - The poetry is a homage to our beloved army men who lost their lives in Indo-China war in 1965. Dead souls wandering in the battlefield ensures the dignity of their lives by a motivating poetry

With our own bloodied colors would inscribe our names in the rocky walls of the nation.

With our own deed colors would engrave our ancestor's fame in the soothe breeze of the nation.

With our own shrouded coffin would cover all wounds till they have healed the soil of our nation.

We would sow the seeds of wisdom & freedom as well thus making lush & green dominion.

We promise to protect you by building

fences with our dried body's skeletons.

We would pave up the road for your feet's to be unharmed with our body's ash.

We would teach you all life lessons with some fine arts.

We would preach the teachings of our Almighty teacher.

We are saviour of the nation & rebel against the anti-nationals.

We are the DEAD.

Some past days ago there we lived

& now we are declared as dead & decomposed.

Our names inscribed on our grave board with "martyr" in top as addressed.

That's enough to rest in peace.

That's enough for the dead souls to glow in.

But promise friends our soul would always be with nation in each & every mission.

THE WELCOME SONG

Prologue - A welcoming song for the young lads of soldiers graduating from National Defence Academy who are all set to serve the national army & country.

You brought a piece of smile that turned all pale faces to chill.

You browsed many books to spread wishes of boon.

You spoke the words of wisdom & truth when you were asked to.

You held your dreams in your heart for you wanted to achieve them soon.

Badge of medals that would splendor up your room.

I wish that this season of bliss would kiss as the brotherhood should.

I wish that God as mason of technology would teach you finer ways to achieve your life's mission.

May you hail up the name of our nation.

The glow worm dances as a goblet of fire.

The rain makes you fresh-up with a bunch of shower.

The clouds gather with a goose of thunders.

The morning blooms with the touch of sun's rays & make you finer.

So, to welcome you my dear soldier.

May your life enlightens with bouquet of flowers.

As the butterflies regain energy with a sip of honey.

So, my friend not only at once feel ever lonely.

'cuz I & our nation is always with you our heroes.

IMPRISON

Prologue – Dated: 1874, A year before a great revolt against the British rule; Peasants around the nation tempting the freedom struggler to gather their voice against the inhuman treatment they have been bearing since their ancestors. They try to ignite the spark of revolution inside the very hearts of countrymen.

Is it not awesome to be seen imprisoned?

It's must be the shame for leading such a life in prison.

Don't you ever will to be freed once again ?

Shameful you should be on your cowardice behavior.

Let your veins burst out from pain.

Hold your breath raise your voice against your's ancestral blame.

Blame that has made your's soul timid.

Let all of us be brave again.

33

Let's not bear any more blame,

for raise your blood against the stain.

No more tolerances to the slave masters.

Gather your breath without making any such whisper.

Let now your reaction speak.

DRILL BEFORE WAR

Prologue – On the dawn of surgical strike, Brave soldiers of country are all set to destroy the enemy's den. A poetic situation is designed to embark the feelings for Uri Avengers.

Moving under chilly night's dark,

Silently we were getting through terror's den without leaving behind any mark.

Sometimes hiding beneath the trees,

at times even crawling under those manned fences such that nobody could track.

Breath ragging in gasps i could only see those tiny stars shivering in clusters.

Even at times thoughts of fright whirling in my mind compelling me to think

"aren't these dummy star's spark?"

Frequent were the scanners of green & laser light red, drones laced with cannons roaming just overhead.

Trees casting their piercing shadows, alike the
nurtured battlefields of meadows.

Hark; I could see those flaming comets projectile
perfectly upright.

Wait! Wait!

Those are false fires thus   pretending terrors
auspicious present.

Instantly aware of the surrounding noted their
movements well.

Learnt their strategies as well, copied every
gesture really fair.

Let's prepare to get off this place, that was the
recall by our troop head.

Memorized every penny of the tit bit & preparing
ourselves to carry out in the next movement made.

Back feet that we would return in proper safety to
our chopper laying farther of our sight.

BETRAYAL FLATTERERS

Prologue –This piece of poetry revolves around a situation that how the countrymen are unified both mentally & heartily for fighting terrorism, Earlier the people have been criticized for trusting again & again blindly the terrorists without taking any action. But now they have to hold their guns tight & fought till their last breath.

Too much patience is portrayed as the act of cowardice.

Too much of tolerance is depicted as the foolish performance.

Despite, why for you cry before such rocky hearts?

'cuz rocks don't weep.

Seeds of stone can't be sowed similarly hyena can never be a herbivore.

Stop chasing those vultures being their slaves.

Ear my words never trust upon those flatterers.

Flatterers are the real enemy of nation brothers.

Deer wanders around in search of the serene fragrance without being aware of the musk hidden beneath it's belly button.

Similarly, we are wandering around the shadows of nightmare for the sake of musk which was lost amidst in uncertain.

Those that of previous worthy years that we spent trusting scavenger as our bestie forgetting all about that scavengers can't ever be trust worthy.

Serpents can't be tamed vultures can't be made pet as well.

Similarly, never trust those faulty cries of cruel.

In those years ahead even mule could have been made knowledgeable but ain't these

envied betrayals.

Country's partition seekers won't be let on mercy.

The answer to the quest of every single bullets out of the terror's gun isn't to bear.

Stop getting poisoned by these mere serpents.

Enough we have bore those terrors now hence it's time to show them the teaser.

Let the world realize what this 56 inched chest can do next.

Treat the terror well-wishers by getting pinched their blisters.

INTERNAL SCAVENGERS

Prologue – The poet here tries to reflect on internal scavengers who is often resembled to the greedy flatterers of the nation who dwells on self-motives & thus loot away the country making it solely weak. So, the nation is at a great risk from these scavengers rather than foreigners.

Cry not sitting helplessly in the hut's corner
thinking of being helped.

Weep not, begging shamelessly from butchers,

thinking of being fetched.

Starve not for being served with stale to eat.

Wish not from the scavengers to faith upon your
deed.

'cuz those are such inhuman disciples of cruelty &
greed.

Who never ever wants freeing our country & get
declared as freed.

These internal scavengers have led our motherland to bleed.

Internal scavengers are alike the vultures & raven who get themselves on carcasses fed.

If at all they are proclaimed as the caretakers of the nation.

Then what shall we expect from them.

These are even duplicates of termites who hollow up the roots by swallowing them.

These can't ever be expected as the well-wishers rather are the contagious blisters.

These blister should be treated well before it's too late.

Be aware of these internal scavengers.

My dear friends of the nation.

Wish of being a voyager against those scavengers.

Roar as such these pity would be dumb.

Act as such these species would be smashed.

Strike them off those that are barriers of the nation "internal scavengers".

Let our own land heals up against the wounds
caused by bloody scavengers.

FIST FULL OF LIFE

Prologue - The poem is a tribute to the men's of a great freedom fighter Tantiya Tope in late 1875's, who led multiple expedition to end the tyrant East India Company's rule, but ultimately failed to achieve their objective. The poetic sayings those men asks the men of country to unite again & fight for their liberty.

A fist full of life that we lived in.

Ultimate liberty that we were ought to give in.

So, we did

in order to raise our flag that has to wave in

Last days of our life that we survived through urging the Almighty to fetch us some more days.

Such that we could at least view our victorious liberalization.

Alas we couldn't make it through.

But promise dear friends & so

What if we are not breathing anymore?

Our soul would rest in peace watching you all in joy's for sure.

If any day at all you are annoyed upon, then be free to taunt us.

But never ever fault yourself.

There may be many to fight across the country but auspicious are those who fight for there countrymen to live in.

So, we did as insisted by our sense.

Thus, constructing protective fence nationwide.

Lend us your long hands to fetch you the ultimate key to liberalization.

ME INDIAN, MY INDIA

Prologue - On the eve of Indian independence, a teen activist shares his joy being liberated with countrymen. Inspired by glorious past & deeds of fellow countrymen. He sings & declares himself proudly to be an Indian.

From night's darkness till the dawn daylight that you caricatured the victorious monarchs.

Whispers of bravery that was earned by your ancestors.

Here has arrived time to sing all along.

Lighting up the candles of hope.

Igniting up the destined fortune.

Blow up the conch of glory.

Fly high & higher that you should sing all around flapping your wings.

Me Indian, My India.

Being dumb from past many years you haven't uttered a single penny.

Now no more let your tongue be hazy.

Here has arrived destined time for you to grab in

& let your voice speak.

Go along with storms, deadly waves

& penetrate across the peak.

Go Chase the voice of glory.

Me Indian, My India.

Come back from past days to presence.

Draw your attention for a newly waiting sunny dawn.

Joyous celeb being

motivation for thousands of people you have to be.

Go! run away, get fetched your dream's sky.

Rulers have exploited you very often.

Even you have been tanned in the farmland under the sun.

You have led your life leaving in wattle den.

Many a nights you have slept empty bellied.

Still soulfully you always stood by side your nation.

Me Indian, My India.

Many floods, storms & quakes arose frequently letting nation's backbone shatter.

But couldn't shear our unity 'cuz that's the one thing really matters.

For we are all Indian, our India.

Spread all through are the colors of cyan.

You are always debted towards the country.

Upon whose land you ate, played, grew elder.

Victory to acquire after numerous defeats you better have learnt.

You are tomorrow's Indian.

Hail the country's name forest, land wide & ocean.

Me Indian, My India.

AWAKENING DREAM

Prologue- A tourist from a foreign land, who has come to visit India, is being welcomed by a local guide He shows her the diverse culture of motherland by singing a song. The tourist then gets fascinated by rich culture of our motherland.

Awakened after a morning dream.

Dream that I saw in the early morning.

Colors of dream scattered everywhere.

Text of arrival brought by the chirruping birds distant from.

Driven by flying mind far away to home alone.

All through from a foreign land.

Being fond of my ritual, custom & culture.

Fragrance of well beingness spread all around the world so full of uprising wonders.

Of new beginning for a new India to reborn.

So, in order to welcome you my dear, dances my
mind with utmost hearty feelings of mine.

Let yours preview of mind reaches sun's shine .

Promise that you would be lost completely in
whirlpool of "skill sculptors".

Even would be fascinated towards the fragrance of
my soil of wonderland.

Such wetful would be the colors of garland.

Enough to garnish up the motherland with diverse
of fragrance.

Colors of festivity would tempt your jive towards
the extremities of this tropical nature.

PATRIOTIC WHISPER

Prolouge – The current poetry is dedicated to Rifleman Jaswant Singh Rawat, MVC who was an Indian Army soldier serving in the Garhwal Rifles. He won the Maha Vir Chakra posthumously as a result of his actions during the battle of Nuranang in present-day Arunachal Pradesh, India, during the Sino-Indian War in 1962.

He was a brave man of the nation who once fought
for his countrymen.

All along with his troop till his last breath was left
all alone.

Not one, not ten instead smashed some 300
intruders of them.

He was a brave rifleman, a cunning warrior among
the most.

He who thus led himself stand still at his post.

Being carefree all about the sun or may be the frost.

All in his vein running was to serve the country
first.

72 hours you kept firing from different bunkers
thus hide seeking with enemies & compelling
them to believe their eyes of having all your war
mates alive.

For this of your brave act of worry

You still owed your position of glory.

Even after your martyrdom, you are still left alive
in register's story.

You thus have proved that a Soldier is never off
duty.

So, for other soldiers as well you own promotion
of different category.

Even you did sacrifice your body leaving all your
soul alive.

It's good that if we are left alive, otherwise our
coffin boxes would return.

Wars aren't won by gun bullets or gunpoint instead
are won for some of the brave warriors like you.

A Saga foretold on their bravely fame who is one
among the thousands name.

He is no other than

" JASWANT SINGH RAWAT".

AZAD

Prologue - The current poetry is dedicated to bravest freedom fighter ever born, Shri Chandra Shekhar Azad. He reorganized the Hindustan Republican Association under its new name of Hindustan Socialist Republican Army (HSRA). A daring freedom fighter and a fearless revolutionary, led some of audacious acts during British rule leaving the Britishers scratching their heads.

Hand that gave splendor to the moustache.

Frown that shivered Britishers at sight.

He was always in for of Freedom's fight.

Red eyes full pledged with threaten that led the Britishers foot tight.

He was an awesome man in formal right.

Indigenous revolver he always held without ever being failed for fair personnel to get them nailed.

Several faulty cases were always made by the fairs against him to get his name blamed.

This that in return kept always a rebel heart in flame.

Let once hail for his name.

The man born former

who is one amongst the thousands of Struggle performer.

He was a lion who dared to fight oneself against those fair butchers.

He took oath of finishing those scavengers if not would finish himself thus sowing the seeds for the future freedom warriors.

Alas! Lastly Fairs took their way & thus proved to be the betrayers.

AZAD better choose to get himself shot with his revolver rather than being caught in the hands of fair scavengers.

BROAD BUILDED CHEST

Prologue- Current poetry reflects about an army personnel who is someone's father but have stayed always in warfare zone far away from home guarding countryside's. The hidden feelings of him is comparably portrayed over in this piece of poetry.

Broad built chest with perfect sight that's what makes him the utmost man of bright.

Leaving far away from home struggles hard for the sake of family which has been an ultimate norm.

Although he too misses his family most but in order alters on casting himself rude.

But this act of altering could easily be caught from his wallet decorated with family snap shot.

He often disclaims as leaving far from home that has become a habit of certain.

Still wetness arises over his eyes beneath his eyelids curtain.

This wetness has some story to be foretold but he better wishes to keep it abide proving himself heavy.

While doing so he has forbidden his beat.

Thus, skin under the shirt has gotten itself tanned.

The feelings of him got themselves all buried underneath his chested grave.

But never ever shares such that his dress doesn't feel guilt.

He gifted us with a royal blued flight by auctioning his smiles.

However, he loves his dress much & we love him so much.

NATION'S GUARD

Prologue - The Border Security Force (BSF) is the primary border defense organization of India. BSF has been termed as the First Line of Defense of Indian Territories. They are charged with guarding India's land border during peacetime and preventing transnational crime. A comparative poetry has been penned down to dedicate them.

Far from home here I have been deployed as fencing guard of the nation.

Here I stand as the warrior son of my country land.

Always in charge of the protection of my country people.

Yes, I am "Nation's guard."

Alert, attentive am always for every war.

I would not allow any intruder underneath the fencing bar.

The uniform that I wear with a fixed star that let's me in a position as a "Nation's guard".

I'm there at penny time for the people's welfare.

A guard not only to the man behind the fencing bar
but also to demons hidden inside the nation's yard.

I grant you consolation to be in safe sleep.

For your Nation's guard is always vigilant & never
off duty.

This country is my home all my duty is to keep it
safe & secure.

MISSILE MAN

*Prologue – This Piece of Poetry is a homage &
tribute to the great President of India 'Dr. APJ
ABDUL Kalam'. A man of worth living led a very
simple but honored life. He is been one of the
finest inspirations for youth in this era.*

God's definitive Creation

A perfect work of art you were,

An uncommon presence on this planet

An individual whom we as a whole appreciate.

The Missile Man of India

On the place that is known for marvels,

Occurred a marvel,

Rocket man of our nation was conceived.

Individuals' leader he was known,

APJ Abdul Kalam was his name.

Clearing a way for youthful age,

In the field of science and innovation.

He enlivened youthful personalities.

He is no more on this planet,

Be that as it may, his spirit hasn't left his homeland.

Opportunity, quality and improvement

were his fantasies.

The day he was conceived,

he committed the day to students.

The sparkle in his eyes,

the grin all over,

What's more, the trust in his intellect,

Moves me and each Indian.

I am proud to be an Indian.

As you are affectionately known,

Your compositions, your lessons

Just a positive beam it has appeared.

You significantly motivated the youthful
personalities

By your significant deeds,

Ascended from a paper dealer to a researcher

You have demonstrated that diligent work never
surrenders.

With all regard we bow to you

For your devotion, be it governmental issues,
compositions or social administration,

A diamond of an individual as you were

NATION'S PROTECTOR

Prologue - The Anti-Terrorism Squad is a special police force in several states of India. The squad has stopped several terrorist attacks in the country. This short piece of poetry is dedicated in the honor of ATS martyrs & its men

A brave chested being as a Nation's guard.

Stood upright far away from farther yards.

Sings the song all along with million new words.

To boost up the voices of many has risen self at the warfare zone of border.

As alike northern pole star will stand still till the last breath lies within self.

I thus promise to be the flag bearer of this estate called "India" till my last breath exists.

So, to raise voices against terror strikes of demons.

Will full-fledged protect every penny being of the nation.

Wave in flag higher & higher than the voices that would resemble as a demarcation of this destined national family.

Hail for the country's name whispers thus to be made as strong amongst the main.

WHEN WILL YOU RETURN!

Prologue - Sorrowing wife's wait for her husband to return from the warfare. Her tender feelings were invoked in this piece of poetry.

The day you went away living my pity heart's mansion all alone.

Eyes sight never allowed the eyelids curtain to fall off.

These feet even don't obey of returning back anymore.

Since the dawn to sunny dusk.

Waits therefore my keen sight anxiously peeping at yours pathway through the midfields of husk.

This short distant road why thus appears too long to be infinite.

"When will you return??"

Only left memento of your memory in forms of medals & awards.

A picture of yours hung on the wall with rewards.

Deeds of your bravery marks higher on the bravery
bill board.

Such brave glorified talks spoken by yours heat
tempered sword.

You were always the one brought forward maybe
it was begin or end of penny war.

Your performance was much keener than eagle &
even faster than the swift bird.

"When will you return dear!"

After-all for you I feel really proud of.

Please accept this tributary salute from your wife.

WHY FOR?

Prologue - Innocent lives were laid down by the acts of terrorism. Inhuman deeds sprouting from the evil minds have put a challenge on this realm. Roots of Humanity is shaken. The Poet asks about the reason for how long this terror would beat us & when we are going to act against them.

Why for? Moral people die sooner.

Why for? Wicked lives longer.

The person ought to laugh, weeps more & the person ought to cry, laughs more.

Enough the inhuman torture we bore.

Enough louder our voices that could roar.

Now no more violence's to be tolerated further more.

This is the country of new generation.

"An eye for thousands eye " that's what our new text is to the terrors brutal leer.

If you stare at us we'll target you in your home.

If you ever dare to we'll send you to the grave dome.

Listen up, hey you! With an open ear.

Now the world will hear our heart's noise.

New we are & are the people with new exaltation.

Thus knowing very properly to cope with each & every situation.

"Be bold, be biased towards the country"

That's what I urge to my countrymen.

HISTORY-PAGES OF PAST

Prologue- This poem piece tries to incase the struggles our ancestors of this soil. They have survived through ages in the form of stories in the pages of a history book.

Borrowing up some colors from histories deserted past,

To thus scribe up some on memories screen.

Turning upon some pages of my ancestral past, found out some pages being stained & dirt wet.

Dust that fled from underneath horseshoes tap, blood that bled into sweat.

Swords that spoke the preaching's of death.

Death that taught us the value of life.

How much of attacks? How much of tortures? That our forefathers bore.

Which caused pages to be worn in mourn?

Courageously stood our ancestors

All across the odds that was brought upon by the enemies from far & forth.

East, west, south & north.

Bravery symbolized flag that waved, singing thus the songs of courage & brave.

Turning again the pages upon some topics of betrayals that was revealed.

Weaponry, howitzer undermentioned on pages are all our tale of struggles that we have survived through.

History's scribed up pages of last salutes the tributes that was made all by our ancestors.

Let's never forget about the root of our origin.

That's what should we all of us mean.

JALLIANWALA

Prologue - The Jallianwala Bagh massacre, also known as the Amritsar massacre, took place on 13 April 1919 when troops of the British Indian Army under the command of Acting Brigadier-General Reginald Dyer fired rifles into a crowd of unarmed Punjabi civilians who had gathered in Jallianwala Bagh, Amritsar. This piece of poetry gives homage & tribute the lives lost in massacre.

Historical dumb proof stays this remarkable
Jallianwala Bagh.

These are those walls that perfectly bore the
echoes of the soary roar.

Blood sits on walls that was spat all over &
everywhere.

A cruel decision that took on hundreds of lives
thus making it a sinful decision taken in freedom's
history ever.

Singing thus the song of history's slandered
episode.

The Act that took place in garden of Jallianwala.

Voices that were lamed with the noise of the gun
bullets.

Continuous rounds of fired brass pellets enough to
burn on the flesh & burst up the bones.

Unmoved, undeterred stands still garden wall as if
explaining history's black moments.

Explaining dark pages of past.

This is the place where thousands breath last.

This was cost of freedom that was repaid for debt.

SOUL ON DUTY

Prologue - Born on 1946 & martyred in 1967 Capt. Harbhajan Singh post he achieved from being only a soldier during 60's. Often considered as The Hero of Nathula, his soul never remained off in duty even served his country land after long of his death. Popularly as Baba Harbhajan.

Every time every trial made it's ultimate with fate of failure.

In the deep thoughts of reason behind, puzzled were pity Chinese soldiers.

These series of failures often tested their courage's valor.

Often incidents & trials of attacks on India kept themselves abide about something reasonably hidden.

Was all these happenings reason of Salvador?

Once a shepherd caught on as suspect when asked about.

"O, Shaahabji" uttering -miraculously reasons
were all 'cuz of the, "soul who stayed paramount".

Astonishment that made its way upon Chinese face
depressed from loud.

Shepherd again, Soul stayed never off duty even
after he's martyred.

If at all any soldier doze off in duty, gets a

slap out from nowhere.

Often, he arrives in Indian soldiers dream to alert
them prior.

All of your plans, movements he foretells them
about to properly nurture in future.

A man riding a white horse   often seen patrolling
in night's scream.

Now has also become trust & faith's stream.

Even fulfills person's wishful shrine.

He held his complete duty as able army man.

Hailed as "Saint Harbhajan".

DARED SOLDIER

Prologue - Lieutenant Manoj Kumar Pandey, PVC, was an Indian Army officer of the 1st battalion, 11 Gorkha Rifles who was posthumously awarded India's highest military honor, the Param Vir Chakra, for his audacious courage and leadership during the Kargil War in 1999. This poetry salutes the brave man of soil.

Wondrous answer given for a quest -

Why you wanted to join "Indian Army"?

In order to get "Paramveer chakra".

Likewise, everybody poses their dream of serving the nation.

But this fellow started preparing since childhood duration.

Battalion Gorkha regiment 1/11 of he was a brave dared Soldier.

With fine touch of perfection could easily grab everyone's stare.

Even asked for to be posted in the conditions worst.

Indeed all he was allowed to lead soldier's squad.

Operation Rakshak owned him as Captain.

Not even bothering a bit of bullets and grenades
from beneath the horizon main.

He ran letting his army men safe stranded hiding
back of a rocky plain.

Even after having iron in chest he held his breath
and successfully conquered the bunkers.

Ah! 3 dots surely got his skull burst.

Fell down courageous lying dead 'no more'.

SARDAR- THE BISMARCK OF INDIA

Prologue - Vallabhbhai Patel (31 October 1875 –
15 December 1950), popularly known as Sardar
Patel. He was an Indian barrister and statesman,
a senior leader of the Indian National Congress
and a founding father of the Republic of India
who played a leading role in the country's
struggle for independence and guided its
integration into a united, Independent nation.
This piece of poetry is a tribute to the Ironman of
India

Being destined farsighted patriot as such was our
Leader.

Influential were his decisions that perfectly met his
patriotic endeavor.

He was one amongst the rare.

Professed by lawyer every instance he worked in
country's favor.

Portrait of "Unity" that he drew.

Sketch of clustered palaces bondage as one that he led grew.

Undivided were states of new India's map.

Best his trial kept everywhere in filling India's gap.

He led himself burnt in volcanoes of non-violence.

Acted as Iron against any offence.

When he raised, voices that roar.

Humble at heart that carried his soar.

"Iron man of India" the knighthood he obtained because of his outstanding courageous dare.

Bardoli Satyagraha movement got titled him as "Sardar".

Such worshipped personnel whom our heart pays peace as tribute.

"Statue of Unity" which is regarded in honor of his salute.

INTO ASHES...

Prologue – Tears are shedding from the eyes of poet as he is standing in the crematory. He has come upon to give his final homage to his childhood friend who was martyred in Ladakh front. Tender & grief-stricken feelings of poet were reflected in this poetry

Spark that turned everything into ashes.

Tomorrow every penny part of his lifeless body will perish into ashes.

Glimpse of hateful mourn would be predicted in those curious faces.

One who used to held flint in his hands is now brooding in the sleepless lap of flint.

Moisty eyes with heart's content into well extinct.

For all those you gave up life.

Some would weep out few drops.

Some would hail out your name in their shouts.

Amidst with garlands of glory.

Some of your friends & neighbor would be
surrounding by-side the body of you.

Alike the earth whirls round the sun.

You will be missed in the collage.

Absence of you in the family photoshoot will be
felt in mirage.

Your acts would be tested in the silence of stage.

Your soul would be greeted into a completely new
phase.

Your ash would nurture "basil " planted just above
your ashes tomb.

Splendored would be concreted dome.

On an endless search operation, you just made
your way out.

Leaving behind yours closest part in an awful wait.

"BAJI"- THE LITTLE BOATMAN

Prologue- Baji Rout is the youngest Indian martyr, having been killed at the age of twelve. Rout, who was a boat boy, was shot by British police when he refused to ferry them across the Brahmani River on the night of 11 October 1938 at Nila kanthapur Ghat, Bhuban, Dhenkanal district. At a very small age who care freely sacrificed his life for the wellbeing of his motherland. This poem reflects his heroism & gives tribute to this forgotten hero.

The courageous story that took place 9 years before Independence date.

This story isn't created or made instead true story of a little patriot "the great"

As fisherman's offspring so was skilled as childish boatman in village's estate.

With grandmom at home "Baji" led his day with boat all alone.

"Boat for a perfect bet but something different was approved for his fate."

The year that stood 1938.

"War of independence" was at it's ultimate peak.

For which regional rulers & common people often met.

Ruler asked people upon to keep a night watch at particular inning.

"Baji" 12th year old raised his voice & urged for himself contributing for the freedom revolt beginning.

Full pledged red eyed "fair butchers" returned after hurting bloodily "Bhuban" village.

They ran off to the banks of Brahmani riverside beach.

In an urgency of escaping they never even hesitated showing their shameful courage.

"Fair butchers" asked the little boatman to get them safely escaped to the opposite bank.

On being asked for "Baji" repeatedly nodded his head to & fro with a big "no".

After believing that all fair efforts getting into mirage.

A "coward fair butcher" shot with a bullet to Baji
on his head.

Ah! Bloodied was the river Brahmani river with
raw blood of a small child.

Weeps motherland 'coz yesterday one who played
in her lap is today laying dead.

LIFE IN DUNGEON

Prologue - A prisoner of war (1971 war) caged in dungeons of enemy state being tortured bluntly & rigorously. But being a well-wisher of his country, he bears all tortures & even promises to be with the nation till his last breath. Unshaken nationalistic motives of prisoner are reflected in this piece of poetry.

Those 20 years of my life that I lived in a caged dungeon.

All was enclosed with a fenced mansion.

Such starving were my days even to get a glimpse of sun.

On the daily basis a new way of torture that was born.

Out of dying for food, a chappati that I was fetched to.

If ever I asked for more, then & their I was fetched with rats to bite me often.

If ever asked for water they used to hit me till I
would sweat upon.

Every penny instant I died for my home & family
who was in almost lone.

Without me they might have been in a state of
Orphan.

Days went on, ages went on

Went on every dusk thus leaving me in an endless
waitful thought.

Whenever I peeped out of my caged fence.

I urge this silent air to send my messages to my
well-wishers ahead.

But all these time i have always lived myself only
for the sake of my nation.

However, I am quite happy for teaching those
"Fair" personnel's a bitter lesson.

Till my last breath I promise to be not letting
suppression worn.

DRESSED AS SOLDIER

*Prologue –This poetry reflects a soldier's duty &
responsibility towards nation who is even ready to
sacrifice his life for our children to have safe
future.*

Dress me up as the soldier,

With stars on my shoulders.

Bring me my patrol cap with emblem over my
forehead that should be.

Hand me revolver or rifle that must be.

I am now ready to pursue my duty in the border.

Let them come O dear!

Be it armed rib enemy or gangs of terror.

I am always ready to show them theirs real mirror.

I would stand still & be my country's flag bearer.

Waving it high up higher & higher till my last
breath should shear.

If ever asked tell my countrymen no need to worry
for.

Theirs's very own nurtured son is standing all the
way as "A Soldier."

From -50°c of Siachen to +50°c of Jaisalmer I
would rely our presence everywhere.

Tell all my nation's future pupils to sleep well
tight.

For tomorrow they have to give their directions to
country's dream flight.

I promise to be hear till I attain

To be called as "Martyr".

If asked about me tell them I am a

"Soldier "who shredded off in darkness of hazy
night.

UNSUNG HERO

Prologue – The Poetry tells about struggles of Shaheed Udhham Singh the unsung hero of the nation. Martyr Udhham Singh (26 December 1899 – 31 July 1940), was a revolutionary best known for his assassination in London of Michael O' Dwyer, the former lieutenant governor of the Punjab in India, on 13 March 1940. The assassination was in revenge for the Jallianwala Bagh massacre in Amritsar in 1919. Singh was subsequently tried and convicted of murder and hanged in July 1940.

21 years since then an event best kept secret underneath the chest.

A revenge for freedom that was well watered with blood.

He was in his late teen while "Jallianwala Bagh's" bloodied act was played.

With deepness of regret that he was left.

With cheapskate labouring the penny savings he made.

Indeed just for a revolver ought to be bought.

21 years of hardship & planning to be turned out
as perfect " rebel".

In the echoes of sacrifices the Struggles that he
faced.

Being true nationalist very well that the country
was served.

Thousands of innocent lives revenge that

his life's last oath perfectly took.

In between many with the sounds of bullets

"Caxton Hall " that shook.

From a blow of therefore becoming a hero.

The journey that was well acted by

"Unsung hero".

BLANKET OF BLUES

Prologue - The poet tries to raise an issue that terror or terrorists are personified in relevance to colors. Unlike Ocean & harsh weathers is specified as enemies in resemblance to colour.

It doesn't take much of time for oceans getting green.

It doesn't take much of time for the weather getting lean.

Only point is that we are rounded with most brine.

I have seen rainbow being created out of nowhere, I mean.

I have seen again those chirrups piercing out from the rainbow fins.

Likewise, colors have unanimous role to play with.

Alike chameleon, suspicious are even colors of ocean so far.

Colors really happen to have mysterious miracles in jar.

Terrorified color has no such defined den or mansion.

Terror often happen to brood underneath the blanket of blues.

Sometimes nested in the ocean or even at times being hidden in web of skies.

Colors of gravy smoke & workout of cruel fireworks can even bloom under plentiful of dawn.

Faulty can even be innocent waves.

Cowardice act of stabbing from back can even be by a mere fawn.

TIME'S FOREHEAD

Prologue - This piece of poetry is dedicated to Shri Atal Bihar Vajpayee ji. He was conferred India's highest civilian honor, the Bharat Ratna, by the President of India. Handled international political pressure like a pro, conducted nuclear tests and passed with flying colours. Many western countries imposed sanctions on India, despite this economy grew in his governance. He is one of the India's finest poets ever produced.

A man surrounded by words.

A well sculpted man of ventures.

Headed amongst the best of poets.

Thus, illustrated as avid reader.

You became the voice of many those.

You blossomed the "lotus" out in the darker noon.

You never ever cared of your escalated foes.

Weaved under the statesmanship of hope.

Yours's such printed gesture carved upon the
time's forehead.

New dreams that were cherished with woven
thread.

Fragments you joined confirming the width.

Life that was fledged in both aspects.

One in "politics" another as a "poet" to be named.

A miraculous child who thus grew out of
blackness into abundance.

A personnel, who drew country's sketch out of
slightness into surplus.

BHOOMI-PUTRA FROM EAST

Theme:- A tribute to the wishful son of the soil "Biju Babu". Bijayananda Patnaik, popularly known as Biju Patnaik, was an Indian politician, aviator and businessman. As politician, he served twice as the Chief Minister of the State of Odisha. The poem reflects his heroics in saving a king of a foreign land from the bondages of seizers.

A kind of war he fought in the hinterlands of

the state.

The kind of imprint that he left in the
countrymen's heart.

Celebrated in millions of heart .

Famed wide for his aviatory flight.

"Dakota" that flew against the odds through
Indonesia for salvation.

A modern "Kharavela" of the new era was born.

Contrived with spectacular abilities that

93

an angel gladiated in the lands of the Russia.

A squall that made it's flight from the deep
horizons of the East.

A conch from the hard oceans that bloomed out of
neat.

The divine land that was blessed to meet it's greet.

He was an envoy in the war fields of "Burma".

With an embedded fountain star the estate was
blessed.

A visionary marvel that he laid for this poignant
nest.

Proverbed as "Biju Babu" in the men's chest.

Alongside the estate's width the poignance flamed
upon when he bloomed into fortunate angel.

The message that met people's prime dazzle.

SAY THANKS TO HIM...

Prologue: A tributary piece of poetry to those defending Line of Control. A pleasant conversation between fellowmen & a soldier is transformed into a poetry

(Mass Chanting)

Say thanks to him who never uttered a single word for.

With a deep smiley face he lost his life indeed, in the insane war.

Please don't shed any tear

for his dead soul lost somewhere far.

(Soldier):

Find someone good enough for my "Fifi" who will love her like I would have ever.

Sorry princess I betrayed keeping promise anymore of tying a better knot with you dear.

Hey stop weeping otherwise I would be annoyed forever.

Could you hear, Fifi?

Hey somebody tell her that I was a nightmare bitter

who showered when the thunders broke out to shear.

If I won't make it back that would be the only reason for I denied to surrender.

O my dad & mom be stronger

never let yourself cry.

Tell my dad that I faced the foes before I could lose my last breathe upon.

Hey common my friends say me Goodbye with hand filled of cheer.

Please don't make your throat soar

Tinny, my sister be stronger enough to recite my brave story.

Hey man don't say it again.

(Mass chanting)

We all know you very well surely you would pull
it without any scratches 'cuz you did it earlier
plenty often.

Say thanks to him who never uttered a single word
for.

With a deep smiley face he lost his life indeed, in
the insane war.

Please don't shed any tear

for his dead soul lost somewhere far.

YOURS PRINCESS

Prologue – A weeping daughter who is unaware of her father's death in border is requesting almighty to return his father to him as soon as possible. Tender feelings of her were transformed into a piece of poetry

I have always been your princess

the sweetest of all the time.

It was all of because you held my little heart.

You would come around & get me my glittered gown.

Surrounding your hand all around, you would be cuddling me under your arm.

I'm daddy's daughter that's what am already therefore.

Hey daddy, I feel very lonely please come home early.

Can't you hear me?

Oh lord, please let the winds fetch me his whisper.

I could feel yours kiss on my fingertips.

You missed my first step & first word beside.

But I know you, 'cuz you still feel the same & for that you many a times weep.

Please come home & do hold us altogether.

Dad hopefully I would be yours forever dear.

But I'm bit annoyed upon you for you became selfish rather.

All you did is for your countrymen for which you fought many war.

All you left was your own family alone which was often shattered with news that got us blown.

All was eyes with ever lasted wet the moment you were gone.

Daddy I have grown up & even I don't stubborn for anymore.

These days I really miss you more.

Mama says you are now that most blinking star.

Can you see me daddy from really very far.

OUR PLACE

Prologue - As the breeze pass by in the eve of warzone, Souls of dead soldiers are whispering about their valor to the countrymen.

Let's mark our place somewhere in the beautiness of sky.

Thus singing the song all along

With a deep sigh very high.

Let the lucks of bravery sing the song with a low toned voice.

From next onwards you would no longer hear our noise.

We are the dead,

short days ago we lived &

Now we lay under the sun's glow being tanned in the daylight warmth.

Sincerely waiting for our turn, to be buried inside this earth.

This death was accepted all by our choice

All for the sake of countrymen rejoice.

Burnt & wounded without the heal, only was the sense of gun trigger that I could feel.

Not being able to shoot tens instead in units which I was capable.

Scarce were the bullets below for all those foes.

Betrayal is the pulse that chocked into the main artery towards the heart.

Thus, letting us to kneel down for depart.

Sorry for I could only make out my life to fail.

With these failing hands I just wish to handover the armory.

Come forward lengthen your hands & be the part of this "art of bravery".

Hold this high take your breath in with a deep sigh.

If you break faith upon us; we shall not sleep in our death bed nigh.

Maybe it's all done with our body.

But our souls shall not sleep neither any tots won't bloom above our burrows until our left mission is complete.

Leave for the country, be for the country.

For every beat that you really owe.

Try harder for every conditions you meet.

Trust me it would be the awesomeness greet in form of gift.

Hopefully you meet yours aspirations indeed, rowing across this fleet.

NETAJI- THE SON OF INDIA

*Prologue – This piece of poetry is a tribute to the
great son of soil 'Subhash Chandra Bose'.
Valiant freedom fighter of nation ever born in
this soil has created Azad Hind Fauj & started an
army coup against the British Empire.*

A pictorial sketch of you hung in my drawing
room in frame.

A book as your biography "Dear Subhash" kept by
side my tea pot on yours name.

In each of my Dad's story you forever stayed as
courageous hero.

Often talks & stories of you has quenched mine
heart of becoming your's devotee.

Dad louds:-

"India needs a person alike Netaji".

Mom whispers :-

"Courageous Subhash's bright nation that should
be".

Grandpa fumbles:-

"Is he alive or dead?".

Upon hearing this my teary eyes seek for region of my hanky.

After you were lost.

Crunchy frunchy news about yours "living or dead" spread whirls all around everywhere.

Down South to upwards the North.

Far East to breadth wards the West.

Many commissions sat for discussions to held.

Sometimes starring at "pir, fakir or saint" thinking them as of you.

Ah! feeling defeated would your well wishers return with face chewed.

You were not constricted as one rather scattered as way of the light rays.

For you to return someday.

Sits by side yours memories of clay.

For sure " you will come one day. "

ODE OF A SOLDIER

Prologue – This piece of poetry revolves around Shaheed Pradeep Panda, Pulwama martyr. In Pulwama on 2017 was on a mission the against the terrorists, who were hiding in a nearby building. He headed his team even got them some, but unfortunately during combat, a terrorist hiding just beneath shot him. Such a valiant personality deserves a poetic salutation.

A son from the mere villa of "Gangpur" with a tempting heart, valour in his chest & raw courage.

All we know the courage he showed against the terror sprinklers those that caught in with

"Pulwama outburst".

He headed his troop & got the terror brothers done.

Ah! but a heated bullet from hidden beneath got his skull chocked.

Tis there he felt dumb stricken.

Waves of tear that took it's way on every single penny eyes.

Numb were paves, girdles over walk way in soar
for their dear is no more.

Trees by side his house worries a lot & misses his
childish touch.

The surrounding that got reverberated with slogans
"Shaheed Pradeep Panda amar rahe" that throttled
air with gaze.

" Gangpur villa" with it's first martyr scribes it's
name in the brave art glories of India.

Martyred son have literally gained the everlasting
alluring fame.

One amongst the millions name.

His castle of pious deeds would be preached
further for other generations to come.

He made the house- proud thus winning the
Dimmy hearts in all at one strike.

Several badges of medals was posthumously
greeted for being amongst the "one alike".

'THE SWORDS OF HINDOSTAN'

Prologue - Outrageous swords men of Rajputana battalion in peaks of Western valley are versing their feelings when war was waged by Mongols in 1200's.

Who says we are craven & cold?
Unworthy the land of our sires.
That our souls worship nothing but for greed & gold.
That quenched are our patriotic fires.
They lie ! For our dear native land,
renowned from all ages afar.
Prepared against all foes we stand.
Our Swords are ready!
'FOR WE ARE THE SWORDS OF HINDOSTAN' !!
Our land is the home of freemen,
it owns neither tyrant nor slave.
To defend it on land or sea,
We have hearts forever ready and brave.
And if ever a despot should dare,
to threaten invasion or war.
We would soon give him cause to beware
of us & our Swords!
'FOR WE ARE THE SWORDS OF HINDOSTAN' !!

'SCORES OF TRIO'

Prologue - This poem is in the memoir of Bhagat Singh, Sukhdev & Rajguru. Their greatness & bewilderness ignited the latent courage inside every right hand activists during mid 1930's.

They felt devoted but undying,

The very gales their names seemed sighing,

The waters murmured the hymns of their names,

The woods were peopled with their fames,

The silent pillar, lone & grey,

Calmed kindered with their sacred clay,

Their spirits wrapped the dusky mountain,

Their memories sparkled over the fountain,

The meanest rill, The mightiest river,

Rolled mingling with their fames forever!

Despite of every yoke Hindostan bears,

The glory for freedom should be always theirs!

& further should be nurtured.

Tis still a watch- word to earth:

Where men of my country would do a deed of worth.

LONG LIVE REVOLUTION

Prologue – Before dying inside walls of cage; An activist from Cuttack pens down some lines on the walls of cage from bloods from his wounded hands as he was thrashed rigorously from distributing anti-British pamphlets in the streets of Cuttack

Aye countrymen! Long live Revolution

Aye countrymen! Long Live Revolution

Unparalleled Revolution

Revolution! Insurgency!

On this side heads for the penance

And eagerness to include,

From that side oppression.

On this side quietness,

Revolution peacefully

Long live Revolution

Revolution! Transformation!

On that side twirly doo. Practice

On this side lack of concern,

On that side naughtiness making

What's more, inordinate boasting?

On this side liquefying of noble hearts.

On that side demonstrations of overbearing

battered with misfits of tart.

It is their doings that will achieve Revolution.

Revolution! Transformation!

On that side demonstrations of persecution

On this side starvation

Source of yearnings.

Are these progressives

Who endure rigors?

Revolution requests rigors

Revolution! Transformation!

Whenever Bhagat, Sukhdev and Guru have

Sacrificed themselves for the country.

Many a man will come to climb the hangman's tree

Without dread and tension.

We need a Revolution

But battle short of rigors,

Revolution of the young.

Glorious Revolution.

Ages past was American Revolution & French
Revolution.

This Revolution of India,

Is the Revolution of the world?

That also was a Revolution

This also is a Revolution

Revolution from each side.

Behold the Revolution is coming,

Aye Countrymen! Long live the upheaval.

Aye Countrymen! Revolution! Upheaval!

LONG LIVE REVOLUTION

A SLEEP IN THE LAP OF MY MOTHER

Prologue – This piece of poetry is based on fictional in which Martyr Bhagat Singh have a conversation with Mother India before getting hanged. This fictional event is transformed into a beautiful poem.

Mother India:

At the point when my 'Moon' vanishes, haziness

Will spread everywhere throughout the world, O individuals!

Bhagat Singh:

O Mother! This 'Moon' of yours

Will light up the entire world out from fears that would rearrange.

Bhagat Singh:

We will swing on the hangman's tree. As individuals do

in swings amid the stormy season.

Mother India:

O Son! Your penance will cut

In two my bonds into sessions.

Bhagat Singh:

O Mother! Give me a chance to suffocate in your
lappet in always harmony.

Try not to keep me alert from getting into
profound rest.

Mother India:

O Son! Your execution will break

the chains of India.

Bhagat Singh:

I will be reawakened again and again

for the freedom of India

Mother India:

O individuals, I reproduced and raised the lion
however

Irwin place him in an enclosure.

Bhagat Singh:

O Mother! At the point when your lion wars

The entire of England will shake.

Give one lion a chance to bite the dust, lakhs of
lions

Will assume birth in his position.

Earth and sky shook when Bhagat Singh

Mounted the gallows.

He took Sukhdev and Rajguru with him and
started

The conclusion to the sufferings of Mother India.